Chichén Itza: The History and Mystery of the Maya's Most Famous City

By Charles River Editors

Picture of El Castillo taken by Daniel Schwen

About Charles River Editors

Charles River Editors was founded by Harvard and MIT alumni to provide superior editing and original writing services, with the expertise to create digital content for publishers across a vast range of subject matter. In addition to providing original digital content for third party publishers, Charles River Editors republishes civilization's greatest literary works, bringing them to a new generation via ebooks.

Introduction

Chichén Itza's Great Ball Court. Photo by Bjørn Christian Tørrissen

Chichén Itza

Many ancient civilizations have influenced and inspired people in the 21st century, like the Greeks and the Romans, but of all the world's civilizations, none have intrigued people more than the Mayans, whose culture, astronomy, language, and mysterious disappearance all continue to captivate people. At the heart of the fascination is the most visited and the most spectacular of Late Classic Maya cities: Chichén Itza.

Chichén Itza was inhabited for hundreds of years and was a very influential center in the later years of Maya civilization. At its height, Chichén Itza may have had over 30,000 inhabitants, and with a spectacular pyramid, enormous ball court, observatory and several temples, the builders of this city exceeded even those at Uxmal in developing the use of columns and exterior relief decoration. Of particular interest at Chichén Itza is the sacred cenote, a sinkhole was a focus for Maya rituals around water. Because adequate supplies of water, which rarely collected on the surface of the limestone based Yucatan, were essential for adequate agricultural production, the Maya here considered it of primary importance. Underwater archaeology carried out in the cenote at Chichén Itza revealed that offerings to the Maya rain deity Chaac (which may have included people) were tossed into the sinkhole.

Although Chichén Itza was around for hundreds of years, it had a relatively short period of dominance in the region, lasting from about 800-950 A.D. Today, tourists are taken by guides to a building called the Nunnery for no good reason other than the small rooms reminded the Spaniards of a nunnery back home. Similarly the great pyramid at Chichén Itza is designated El Castillo ("The Castle"), which it almost certainly was not, while the observatory is called El Caracol ("The Snail") for its spiral staircase. Of course, the actual names for these places were lost as the great Maya cities began to lose their populations, one by one. Chichén Itza was partially abandoned in 948, and the culture of the Maya survived in a disorganized way until it was revived at Mayapán around 1200. Why Maya cities were abandoned and left to be overgrown by the jungle is a puzzle that intrigues people around the world today, especially those who have a penchant for speculating on lost civilizations.

Chichén Itza: The History and Mystery of the Maya's Most Famous City comprehensively covers the history of the city, as well as the speculation surrounding the purpose of Chichén Itza and the debate over the buildings. Along with pictures and a bibliography, you will learn about the Maya's most famous city like you never have before, in no time at all.

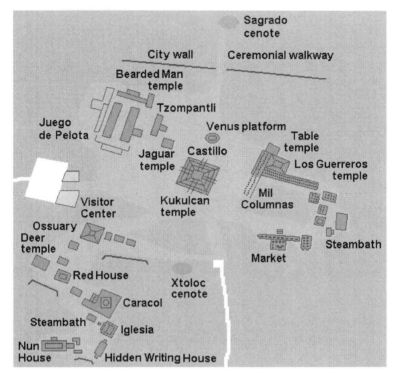

The layout at Chichén Itza

Every year, on the days of the Autumnal and Vernal Equinox, crowds gather at the base of the Castillo, the spectacular stepped pyramid at the heart of the Mayan city of Chichén Itza. Slowly, over the course of the day, the shadows cast by the pyramid's corners seems to slither down the balustrade of the principal stairway. This ancient site, whose construction was perhaps performed around the same time of the first great Gothic cathedrals of Europe, was dedicated to the serpent god Kukulkan, a connection which seems to give meaning to the twice-a-year appearance of the snake[1].

---

1   "The Sunlight Effect of the Kukulcán Pyramid or The History of a Line" by Tomás Garcia-Salgado. In the *Nexus Network Journal*. Accessed online at: http://perspectivegeometry.com/sitebuildercontent/sitebuilderfiles/kululcanpg.pdf on 1 Oct 2013.

Photo of the serpent effect at El Castillo during the spring equinox in 2009

The serpent effect at night using artificial light. Photo by Bjørn Christian Tørrissen.

While El Castillo is the most distinctive building on the site, Chichén Itza was far more than simply a ceremonial center. In fact, it was one of the most visually spectacular and important cities economically, politically and culturally during the period of Mayan history known as the Postclassic, making it arguably the mightiest city ever built among the Mayans, and dwarfing the earlier regional "superpowers" of Tikal and Calakmul.

The city's size and obvious power has attracted archaeological attention for decades, and that work is ongoing as more of the site is excavated, but Chichén Itza is also unique among other sites in Mesoamerica for the way it fused Mayan art and architecture with styles coming from the Toltec peoples around the area north of what is today Mexico City. While early archaeologists theorized that Chichén Itza might have been an eastern capital of an empire originating in the Toltec capital of Tula (the equivalent of considering Chichén to be the Byzantium to Tula's Rome), these theories have found little support in the archaeological record. Today, scholars tend to believe that the Toltec influence was based on trade and religious links. Regardless of the source, this Toltec influence fused with earlier Puuc Mayan forms to create unique art and a cosmopolitan city where goods, ideas and people from across Mesoamerica met.

The Tzompantli ("Skull Platform") at Chichén Itza displays skulls impaled vertically on the wall, a style influenced by the Toltec. Photo by Bjørn Christian Tørrissen.

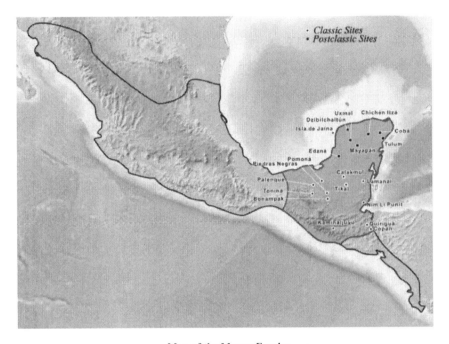

Map of the Mayan Empire

The Mayan world is divided amongst the Lowlands of the Yucatán peninsula (Mexico's answer to Florida, jutting into the Gulf of Mexico) and the Highlands of today's Guatemala, and the Mexican state of Chiapas. Chichén Itza is firmly located in the Lowlands, close to the northern Gulf shore. Unlike Florida, which is in essence a glorified sand bar, the Yucatán is set on firm bedrock: a broad shelf of limestone and similar rocks called the Yucatán Shelf. Covering the Peninsula is a thick tropical rainforest that is home to species like the tapir, jaguar, toucan, and scarlet macaws. This geology means that there are almost no topographically distinguishing marks on the landscape, so the pyramids of the ancient cities and the church spires of the new ones are the only break to the endless green monotony. Driving west from the modern tourist city of Cancún to the ruins of Chichén Itza, visitors cross a very flat landscape on arrow-straight roads that seem to run through an endless canyon of jungle green.

The geography of this landscape defines much of what was (and still is) possible agriculturally and socially. Rainforests concentrate nutrients in the bodies of trees, leaving the soils relatively thin and por, meaning the Mayans who lived in the area could benefit from the normal rainforest agricultural technique of swidden.[2] To understand better the techniques of the ancient residents of Chichén Itza,

---

2   Swidden agriculture, previously called "slash-and-burn" agriculture involves the cutting and burning of a small area of the rainforest and then using the ashes as fertilizer for several seasons of crops. However, fertility gained by this way is

one need look no further tan the contemporary Mayan community of Cobá, living to the south and west of the ruins[3]. The residents of Cobá live densely packed into a small central town much smaller than Chichén Itza, with small outlying settlements of a handful of buildings in the forest. The community of Cobá owns the surrounding forest communally, and a farmer's council divides up land into *milpas*, fields which the individual then clears. Once cleared, the farmer searches the thin soil for places where the subsoil limestone is worn away into a soil-filled hole and then plants corn and other crops into these holes, with different crops needing holes of differing depths. This gives the *milpa* a disorganized appearance, with crops scattered apparently randomly across its area.

Archaeologist Ellen Kintz, who studied these contemporary Maya, has argued that the ancient Yucatecan cities like Chichén Itza would have functioned in much the same way, only on a much wider scale. As the crops could never be planted densely, they had a need for a wide area to support the urban core, a reality which added to the Mayan system of scattered independent city-states.[4] Mayan farms produced a variety of crops, the staples being corn or maize with beans and squashes. In some Maya communities, cotton, cocoa and honey were produced, and whatever wasn't used for basic living was traded. Along the coast of modern Belize, Maya agricultural practices included the use of irrigation ditches, mounded fields and reclamation of swamp land. These techniques would have ensured a very long period of productivity for agriculture.

Just as modern Mexico has found it easy to construct straight highways across the jungle, so too did the ancient Maya. In fact, many of their highways, which were elevated above the surface of the jungle floor on a terrace-like structure, still exist today. They fanned out from Chichén Itza and her sister cities, not only connecting the different city-states but also serving to connect the agricultural outlands with the core settlements. These roads allowed farmers to walk to and from their fields every day, since the Pre-Columbian Mesoamericans had no domesticated pack animals.

The urban core of Chichén Itza was, at its height, roughly 15 square miles (or 25 square kilometers), making it roughly half the size of the New York City borough of Staten Island. Most of this ruin remains covered with rainforest today, so only the core structures - roughly analagous to the National Mall in Washington D.C. - has been cleared and restored. These outer areas would have been characterized by buildings in the pole and thatch style: a framework of poles set into the ground, with walls made of branches between them which gave privacy but also allowed for breezes to enter. The roofs were thatched with local grasses. However, in increasingly wealthier districts of the city, there is a greater percentage of stone buildings, which had the distinct advantage of being relatively impervious to the hurricanes that too often sweep across the region.

---

quickly used up and the swidden farmer must then move on to other sites - often moving his or her entire settlement to uncut territories. The Mayans would never have been able to build stable, long-term cities if they used up the soil in this way in the span of a few years.

3   Though we must always take care while making such comparisons, as obviously much has changed in the centuries since the fall of Chichén Itzá and the present day - perhaps most significantly the destruction of the Mayan religio-political system and its replacement by first Spanish and then Mexican dominance of the region. However, today's Maya do work under the same geographical and climatological constraints and so some careful comparisons can be made.

4   *Life Under the Tropical Canopy: Tradition and Change Among the Yucatec Maya* by Ellen Kintz (1990). Case Studies in Cultural Anthropology.

The buildings were arranged into compounds, which were probably associated with extended families. Compounds included a number of buildings, one of which was a kitchen (removed from the others to protect against the threat of fire), and an open area that probably had small vegetable gardens and tres for fruits, nuts, and fuel. However, unfortunately little is known about the lives of these "suburbanites" and their neighborhoods, as almost all archaeological attention at the site has been focused on the spectacular ceremonial core.

When the Yucatán is blesssed with rainfall, the porous nature of the underlying limestone (the same porousness that allows for the *milpa* style of cultivation) means that almost all of the water is absorbed into the bedrock, so the Peninsula has almost no surface water sources, whether lakes or rivers. This was true of Chichén Itza, which is not located on a river or lake. Instead, the citizens drew their water primarily from two great open sinkholes called *cenotes*. *Cenotes* were considered to be sacred, so sacred that one of the cenotes at Chichén Itza was used only for ritual purposes and is today called the Sacred Cenote. The Sacred Cenote is located to the north of the city center and was connected to it by a ritual causeway. Residents offered precious goods here to the rain god Chaac, who is still sometimes invoked by nearby residents, in hopes of rain and good harvest[5]. The other water source, Cenote Xlacah, probably served as the primary well for the citizenry[6].

Photo of the Sacred Cenote by Emil Kehnel

All Mayan cities had a ceremonial core, the district of grand stone buildings and broad courtyards at the heart of the city that served as the religious, political, military and probably economic focal point of the city. This district was also the organizing nexus for the entire city-state and the place where the governing elite demonstrated their wealth and power in works of art and elaborate ritual. The ceremonial core of Chichén Itza was located a few hundred yards to the south of the Sacred Cenote,

5   "A Tour of Chichen Itza with a Brief History of the Site and its Archaeology" by Jorge Peréz de Lara. Accessed online at: http://www.mesoweb.com/chichen/features/tour/index.html on 1 Oct 2013

6   "Archaeological Survey at Chichen Itza" by George F. Andrews of the University of Oregon. Accessed online at: repositories.lib.utexas.edu. Pg 3.

and it has been divided by historians into two parts: an older section to the south consisting of styles similar to the Puuc Maya tradition of surrounding cities and a younger, grander section to the north which emulates styles from the Toltec city of Tula far to the west.

Dominating the north is the spectacular symmetrical pyramid El Castillo, which is actually only the outermost layer of a pyramid that was expanded several times over the city's long history.[7] Meanwhile, other principal buildings of ancient Chichén Itza included the Tzompantli (or Skull Platform), the Temple of Jaguars, the Temple of Warriors, the Caracol and the Nunnery. It is immediately apparent that most of these names were applied by the Spanish Conquistadores (such as El Castillo) or English-speaking archaeologists who created names based on physical description (such as the "Red House" near the Caracol) or by guessing its function (like "The High Priests' Temple" at the north end of the southern group).

The High Priests' Temple

The Caracol[8] is almost as famous as El Castillo itself, and it has also attracted interest for decades. The name is Spanish for "snail," a term that comes from a spiral staircase within the structure's central turret, which looks something like a snail-shell when looked at from above. Like many Mayan buildings, the Caracol was constructed on a broad stone platform, and the structure rises above its neighbors, dominating the southern complex of buildings. The most prominent feature of the Caracol is the circular tower at the top of it. While much of the tower has fallen over the centuries, the remaining walls have windows which appear to have functioned as siting guides for ancient observers tracking the Sun and the planet Venus, crucially important celestial features for the Maya. A document called the Dresden Codex from roughly the same time period as Chichén Itza's glory days describes Venus as

---

7   "Chichén Itzá" in *Exploring Mesoamerica* by John M.D. Pohl (1999). Oxford University Press. Pgs 118-131.
8   This should not be confused a Mayan site in modern-day Belize that is today known as "Caracol," a site of considerable importance which was larger than Belize City and held a population greater than Belize itself.

Chak Ek', or "The Great Star." It appears to have been seen as the harbinger of war, death and victory. Battles between the mightiest cities (of which Chichén Itza was certainly one) were described as "Star Wars," certainly a reference to Chake Ek' and other stars whose motions may have been carefully tracked at the Caracol.[9] The Grolier Codex, which was written around 1230 A.D., and the Dresden Codex, written just before the Spanish conquest, have tables for the plotting of the phases of Venus, Mars, and solar eclipses.

Photo of the Caracol by Daniel Schwen

---

9   "Venus: The War Star" in *The Chronicle of the Mayan Kings and Queens: Deciphering the Dynasties of the Ancient Maya* by Simon Martin and Nikolai Grube (2000). Thames and Hudson. Pg 16. "El Caracol: A Maya Observatory" at the Virginia University Astronomy Department, accessed online at: http://www.astro.virginia.edu/class/oconnell/astr121/el-caracol.html

Photo of the observatory by Bruno Girin

Another important feature of the center was the Grand Ballcourt. The Mesoamerican ballgame was a combination of sporting event and religious ritual that was practiced not only throughout the Mayan region but up through what became the Aztec Empire, spreading from modern-day Nicaragua even all the way north to modern-day Arizona. In most Maya cities that have been excavated, there is at least one ball court, indicating the central importance of the game now referred to as pok-ta-pok. The long rectangular structures with sloping or vertical walls along the sides were the sites of a game in which two teams of 2-7 people moved a rubber ball by hitting it with the body without the use of hands or feet. The most effective method of directing the ball was through the use of the hips. The goal was to pass the ball through a vertical circular ring attached to the long wall of the court.

This game or a variant of it was important in several Mesoamerican cultures, but based on the archeological evidence the Maya considered it to be a central feature in their urban life. The game played such a central role in courtly life that one of the common titles for a Mayan king was "aj pitzal" ("ballplayer").[10]" Moreover, sculptures associated with ball courts suggest that the game concluded with ritual human sacrifice, presumably captives, although some have suggested that the losing team or the captain of the team were treated to sacrificial execution. This procedure makes sense in the light of the theory that the game was a way of settling municipal grievances or inter-city wars. If the game was merely played for the sake of entertainment and competition, a ritual sacrifice of the losers would have been a rather severe method of improving the quality of play.

The stone ring at the Grand Ballcourt in Chichén Itza was nearly 30 feet off the ground. Photo by Kåre Thor Olsen.

At Chichén Itza, archaeologists have found the largest known Ballcourt in the world. Shaped like a capital "I," it was 140 meters (470 feet long) with a width of 35 meters (115 feet). The walls around it, where the hoops were located, are 10 meters high (32 feet). Around these walls are six sets of stone panels, carved with bas relief images of ballplayers girded in armor resembling something between a modern American football player and a full-out Mayan warrior[11]. Nowhere else have archaeologists found such a vast playing ground, leading many to surmise that the "game" was more pageant than sport here. Undoubtedly, it was seen by the city's elites as crucially important to their power structure, or they otherwise would have never invested such engery in its infrastructure.

10 "The Royal Culture of the Maya" in *The Chronicle of the Mayan Kings and Queens: Deciphering the Dynasties of the Ancient Maya* by Simon Martin and Nikolai Grube (2000). Thames and Hudson. Pg 15
11 "Chichén Itzá" in *Exploring Mesoamerica* by John M.D. Pohl (1999). Oxford University Press. Pgs 123-124.

Photo of the Grand Ballcourt taken from El Castillo. Photo by André Möller

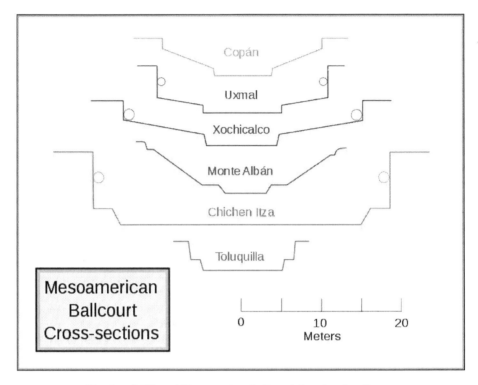

The size of different Mesoamerican ballcourts based on locations

Chapter 2: Origins of Chichén Itza

The precise origins of any great ancient city will probably be forever buried archaeologically under the weight of later construction and historically under the weight of later mythologizing. This is no doubt the case with Chichén Itza, but while scholars may never be able to determine where and when the first ballgame was played at Chichén Itza, they can piece together an understanding of why this particular city rose to prominence at the time it did.

The apogee of Mayan culture and influence was in the period known to Mesoamerican scholars as the "Classical" period. Ranging from to the 3rd-9th centuries, during this time the región was dominated by two great powers, Tikal and Calakmul, located far to the south of the Yucatán in the northern Highlands. To the west, central Mexico was dominated by the cities of Teotihuacan, Cholula and Monte Albán. This was a period of relative stability, though it probably didn't feel that way as the ruling dynasties of Tikal and Calakmul vied for power and fought numerous proxy wars through their many client states[12]. This period is comparable to the great "cold war" between Athens and Sparta in ancient Greece.

The name "Chichén Itza" translates to "near the edge of the well of the Itzaes", which refers to at least one of the city's two cenotes. The cenotes certainly served as the primary reason for the city's placement, because sources of secure water are rare on the Peninsula and were thus greatly treasured by the locals. While the rainforest appears lush and water-filled, the porous nature of the bedrock means that stable sources of water are as precious here as they might be in a more overtly dry climate, and this also explains the enduring importance of the rain god Chaac for the Yucatecan Maya. Manuscripts date the settlement's founding at either 415-435 A.D. or 455 A.D., but either way they appear to agree on the rough date of origin. This means that the city was founded at roughly the same time the Anglo-Saxons conquered Britain and Atilla was ravaging the European mainland. These dates fit well within the Classic period of Mayan history, but for centuries, the city was a small, little-known backwater[13].

The Classic period ended throughout Mesoamerica at roughly the same time, and it has been argued that this was due to climate changes. Certainly, the old polities were no longer able to hold onto power, and throughout Mesoamerica great empires crumbled and were replaced by numerous smaller states. Amongst the Maya, the collapse of this period affected the Highlands, so the center of Mayan culture moved north onto the limestone shelf of the Yucatán Peninsula, to cities like Mayapá, Uxmal, Tulum, Cobá and, most importantly, Chichén Itza. This was also a period of great movements of people and ideas across Mesoamerica; while there have always been pan-Mesoamerican trends (such as the Ballgame), this period saw people moving at unprecedented rates. One of the eventual outcomes of this movement was the Toltec influence on Chichén Itza (discussed further in depth in a later chapter), and more generally, it brought rapid growth to the cult of the feathered serpent, the god Kukulkan, who was called Quetzalcoatl amongst the Aztecs. This cult would eventually be centered on Chichén Itza, and its importance was paralleled by the city's rise in stature.

12 *The Atlas of World Archaeology* by Paul G. Bahn (ed.) (2009). The Brown Reference Group Ltd. Pgs 170-171.
13 "Pre-Hispanic City of Chichen Itza" at the UNESCO World Heritage List, accessed online at:
   http://whc.unesco.org/en/list/483

El Castillo's base depicts Kukulkan on the west face of the northern stairway.

However, in its earliest days, Chichén Itza was part of a larger subgroup of Mayan cities called the Puuc in the north of the Peninsula. The center of the distinctive Puuc architecture was the city of Uxmal, which was located to the west of Chichén Itza. Puuc style was characterized by restrained, carefully ordered ornamentation. The buildings had smooth, stucco finishes and were often dominated by broad horizontal lines and building elements[14].

There are some elements of oral history that have survived amongst the Maya people describing the foundation of Chichén Itza. The ruler of the city was known as the Itza, but the word "Itza" is actually a blurry one. While it appears in the city's name and the ruler's title, it is also used for the ethnic group that eventually dominated the city and survives in a remnant in northern Guatemala. Moreover, in oral legend the term also refers to the name of a caste of warriors from the nearby city of Mayapán (also a Puuc city) who rebelled against the Cocom (the title of Mayapán's priest-king) and fled Mayapán to found Chichén Itza. It is possible that this caste then became an ethnicity over time and lent its name to both city and ruler. The legends also maintain that these Itzaes claimed descent from the god Kukulkan, but this was probably a later addition to the story, since the early city did not appear to be dedicated to Kukulkan but Chaac, the pan-Mayan rain god. The legend goes on to state that 120 years later, the Cocomes of Mayapán conquered Chichén Itza, overthrew the Itzaes, and made the city a dependency of their state[15].

---

14 "Uxmal" in the *Encyclopedia Britannica*, accessed online at:
  http://www.britannica.com/EBchecked/topic/620988/Uxmal#ref225521
15 *The Myths of Mexico and Peru* by Lewis Spence. 1913 (2005). Barnes and Noble Books. Pg 133.

There is nothing implausible about these stories, though even if they are true, they only tell a portion of the story: the elite tale of war, rebellion and conquest. This tale does not explain why Chichén Itza, amongst all of the tiny statelets that emerged in the chaos of the Postclassic Transformation, rose to become the mighty state and the Maya's most famous city. Archaeological evidence shows that as Cobá (the regional center in the Classic period) declined, Chichén Itza and Uxmal (both in the west) rose up as allies or sister-cities to fill the gap. The Lord Chaak (ruler of Uxmal) expanded on land, while Chichén Itza sought to capitalize on sea-going trade, and what the Itzaes brought to the trading table was salt, a vitally important and difficult-to-acquire nutrient. While today people think of salt as an everyday commodity, in the ancient world it was a rare and expensive commodity, hence the English expression "worth his weight in salt". Chichén Itza controlled a coastal port named Isla Cerritos and one of the largest saltworks in Mesoamerica, called Emal[16].

During this period, the Itzaes built a ceremonial center in the core of the city that in many ways was typical of the surrounding Puuc centers. Today many of these buildings survive and make up the Southern Group of the ceremonial core. The most famous of these structures is the Caracol, an observatory similar to a building in Uxmal. The Caracol is decorated with images of the hook-nosed rain god Chaac, and all around it are other smaller buildings also done in a Puuc style, including the Red House, the Temple of the Lintels, and the House of the Deer[17]. They have the same austerity and dominant horizontal architectural elements as buildings in Uxmal, and furthermore, dates found on inscriptions of a set of buildings called the Nunnery Group in this complex date back to 875-880 A.D., during the heyday of Uxmal[18] and before the 10th century rise of the cult of Kukulkan and the Toltec influence. Thus, these structures come from an era when Chichén Itza would have been a young, up-and-coming power, allied to but probably still under the shadow of Uxmal.

---

16 "Chichén Itzá" in *Exploring Mesoamerica* by John M.D. Pohl (1999). Oxford University Press. Pgs 128-129.
17 "Chichén Itzá" in *Exploring Mesoamerica* by John M.D. Pohl (1999). Oxford University Press. Pgs 126-127.
18 Dated as the reign of Lord Chaak: 875-890 AD.

Picture of the Red House taken by Régis Lachaume

As a result, by combining the archaeological record and oral history, scholars can piece together a probable origin for Chichén Itza. A group of warrior rebels called the Itza from Mayapán (or perhaps another city lost to time) fled their city and either founded or conquered a small settlement near the coast which they named for themselves. In the chaos of the early Post-Classic, they allied themselves with an older dynasty in the neighboring city of Uxmal and their famous king Lord Chaak, after which they started emulating th Uxmal elites' Puuc architectural style. The Itzaes specialized in seaborne trade and salt mining, carving out an increasingly lucrative niche for themselves, and though they may have been conquered temporarily by their former overlords, this does not halt their growing commercial success or their connections with exotic societies across the Gulf of Mexico. In fact, it is foreign influence, primarily from the Toltecs of Central Mexico, that would forever reshape the city.

Chapter 3: The Arrival of Toltec Influence

As the Postclassic period began in earnest, the neighboring city of Uxmal began to decline. By 925 A.D., all of the central buildings of this other city were abandoned, along with most of the other Puuc centers. Uxmal was not forgotten - the powerful Xiu family would view it as their place of origin and venerate its shrines until the Spanish Conquest - but it was forever eclipsed. Mayapán would continue under the Cocomes until the Spanish Conquest, though it also did not ascend again in the Postclassic period. By the late 900s, the only power left in the region was Chichén Itza[19].

While Chichén Itza began its rise by controlling the local trade in salt, it began to diversify as it was drawn into a trade network dominated at the time by its eventual sister-city Tula, the capital of the Toltec peoples. The Toltec are one of the most famous Mesoamerican groups, but they are also the most controversial and mysterious. The Toltec have been identified as the group that established a strong state centered in Tula, and the Aztec claimed the Toltec as their cultural predecessors, so much so that the word Toltec comes from the Aztec's word Tōltēcatl, translated as artisan. The Aztec also kept track of the Toltec's history, including keeping a list of important rulers and events, that suggest the peak of the Toltec occurred from about 900-1100 A.D.

However, unlike the Mayans, the Aztecs are not widely viewed or remembered with nuance, in part because their own leader burned extant Aztec writings and rewrote a mythologized history explaining his empire's dominance less than a century before the Spanish arrived. Thus, even as historians have had to rely on Aztec accounts to trace the history and culture of the Toltec, they have had to deal with the fact that the evidence is fragmentary and incomplete. Given the fact that the Aztec leaders engaged in revisionist history, it becomes even more difficult to be sure that the Aztec accounts of the Toltec are accurate, with some scholars going so far as to call the Toltec culture nothing but myth.

While scholars continue to debate whether the Toltec were an actual historical group, there is an added layer of mystery to the fact that the settlement at Tula has a lot in common with Chichén Itza. The architecture and art at both sites are so similar that archaeologists and anthropologists have assumed they had the same cultural influences, even as historians struggle to determine the historical timelines, and thus whether Tula influenced Chichén Itzá or vice versa.

The Toltecs were masters at long-distance trade, and they controlled numerous sea routes across the Gulf of Mexico, bringing obsidian and turquoise down from the deserts of what is today northern Mexico and the U.S. Southwest.[20] Meanwhile, from the southern region of what is today Guatemala and Nicaragua, the Itzaes brought up gold and cacao, and they began to grow cotton locally. Evidence of the great extent of this network has been found in Pueblo Bonito, a 9th-12th century settlement in Chaco Canyon in the northwestern corner of today's New Mexico. A major site inhabited by the ancestors of today's Puebloan peoples, it was the final terminus of trade routes that began far to the south of Chichén Itza. The locals mined turquoise and tanned buffalo hides for trade, and one of the most important items they bought were massive quantities of vivid red macaw feathers carried up from Central America. At least some if not the great majority of these feathers would have passed through the markets of Chichén Itza and the city's port on their journey north[21].

During this period, Chichén Itza was probably viewed by its neighbors as a cosmopolitan center, a place where one might encounter people from strange cities across the seas, from the legendary deserts of the far north, from the fallen mountain kingdoms of the southern Maya, or the strange jungles of the deep south. With the possible exception of the great Toltec city of Tula to the north, there was, for the

---

19 "Uxmal" in *Exploring Mesoamerica* by John M.D. Pohl (1999). Oxford University Press. Pgs 106-117.
20 A form of black volcanic glass that is perhaps the finest quality stone for the making of stone tools, but is only found in a handful of locations in Mesoamerica.
21 "Mesoamerican Themes and Chaco Canyon" by F.J. Mathien (1997). Accessed online at:
http://www.colorado.edu/Conferences/chaco/mesomod.htm

Mesoamericans, no place on Earth quite like Chichén Itza.

Precious stones were not the only import from central Mexico. As the other Puuc cities declined or disappeared around Chichén Itza, the future metropolis began to track its own unique course. Somewhere in the 9th century, the city's rulers began to consciously, actively, and at great cost import a series of cultural, religious, political and architectural innovations from their trading partners in Tula. Perhaps the most important import of this period was the worship of the god Kukulkan. The name "Kukulkan" means the "Feathered Serpent," the same meaning of his Toltec name "Quetzalcoatl." He was associated with jade stones, the creator of humanity (through the sacrifice of his own blood), and the giver of maize to his creations. He was said to have been tricked into committing incest with his sister and set himself on fire out of remorse after he learned the truth. He then rose to heaven and became Venus, which as already noted was extremely important to the early Itzaes who built the Caracol. Other legends held that he crossed the sea on a boat, promising to return in the future[22], the very legend Hernan Cortes would utilize to his advantage when conquering the Aztec

The ancient Mesoamericans had a worldview which was relatively flexible when it came to the addition of gods and other supernatural beings to their pantheons. Even Christianity was absorbed by the Maya as yet another divinity, and today Yucatec shamans are comfortable extorting the rain god Chaac in one breath and the Virgin Mary in the next. Thus, Kukulkan was probably worshiped alongside other deities on the Peninsula without too much anxiety, and it was probably inevitable that the cult of the Feathered Serpent would enter the Mayan region through the port city of Chichén Itza.

However, what is surprising is that it the Itzaes appear to have wholeheartedly accepted Kukulkan as their deity and made their city the center of his worship throughout the Mayan lands. This is most evident in the construction of El Castillo, which apparently served as the Temple of Kukulkan in the new, Toltec-influenced northern section of the urban core. Unquestionably one of the most impressive monuments in ancient Mesoamerica, El Castillo is a square structure that runs 60 meters (190 feet) on each side and reaches a height of 12 meters (40 feet). It is built in a step-style, like the Mesopotamian ziggurats or early Egyptian pyramids, but not like the smooth surfaces of later Egyptian pyramids, such as those at Giza. At the center of each of the four sides is a broad staircase, and modern climbers quickly discover the remarkable steepness of the staircase and the narrowness of the stairs themselves, which require the climber to often turn his or her feet sideways for a good footing and sometimes to lean forward, scrambling on not just feet but also hands. This was probably intended, as it would cause the devotee to clamber up in a semi-prostrate position before the might of Kukulkan.

El Castillo is also much broader than the typical Mayan pyramids, giving it a squat profile that is reminiscent of pyramids found around Central Mexico in places like Cholula, Tula, Teotihuacan and Tenochtitlan. The Maya often built their pyramids in stages, by sheathing a preexisting pyramid in a new layer of stone, burying the old one, and thereby creating a taller, broader replacement. Excavations by the Mexican government in the 20th century found two smaller pyramids subsumed

---

22 "Kukulkan" and "Quetzalcoatl" at the *Encyclopedia Mythica*. Accessed online at: http://www.pantheon.org/. "Kukulcan" at the *Mythology Dictionary*. Accessed online at: http://www.mythologydictionary.com/kukulcan-mythology.html

within the current exterior. These older pyramids appeared to blend the Mayan and Toltec influences more than the last incarnation, which does away with the hybrid styles and predominantly favors the Toltec elements.[23]

The north side of El Castillo

El Castillo was only one of a large number of Toltec-influenced buildings[24]. Near the Castillo is the Tzompantli, a low platform decorated with images of jaguars and eagles. It has no antecedents in Mayan architecture, but it's remarkably similar to the Tzompantli in Central Mexico, which held wood scaffolds that were used to display the decapitated heads of opponents. Chichén Itza also has a Temple of the Warriors, famous for its elaborate colonnades and still covered in carvings of dramatic Toltec-style warriors[25].

23 "Chichen Itza" in *Exploring Mesoamerica* by John M.D. Pohl (1999). Oxford University Press. Pgs 121
24 "Chichen Itza and the Toltec Question" in *The Chronicle of the Mayan Kings and Queens: Deciphering the Dynasties of the Ancient Maya* by Simon Martin and Nikolai Grube (2000). Thames and Hudson. Pg 229.
25 "Chichen Itza" in *Exploring Mesoamerica* by John M.D. Pohl (1999). Oxford University Press. Pgs 122-124

The Temple of the Warriors. Photo by Keith Pomakis

The Temple of the Warriors' columns

Statue of Chaac Mool located at the Temple of the Warriors. Photo by Bjørn Christian Tørrissen.

However, perhaps the most striking difference for the Maya themselves cannot be easily seen architecturally. Chichén Itza had no King, despite the fact kingship was the definitive element of the Classic Mayan polity. The relationship between the king and the gods on the one hand and the king and his subjects on the other lay at the heart of Mayan politics; the king was seen to make sacrifices - often of his own blood - in order to please the gods and continue to bring their blessings down on the city. When the king failed in his duties and the gods were displeased, their boons - like regular rainfall - were withdrawn. The kings were also considered to be the high priests of the patron gods of the cities. Much of Mayan art, history and architecture is focused upon the personage of the king and his family, their ancestors and their glorious deeds.

Conversely, the Toltec leaders of Tula did not inherit their power through their family genealogy. Instead, they were elected by other elites (the heads of important families) and confirmed by the high priests of the two most important gods, one of which was Quetzalcoatl/Kukulkan. It appears that the government of Chichén Itza was similarly organized, because there are no references to the dynastic origins of leaders and many inscriptions are puzzlingly free of reference to a king altogether, something unheard of at earlier Mayan sites. There are also no references to leaders as "brothers" or "companions." This has led scholars to theorize that Chichén Itza may have been a confederacy of powerful families dedicated to the worship of Kukulkan. Perhaps this institution, which was obviously inspired by that of the Toltecs, emerged from the early Itza warrior brotherhood, or it may have been made up of local elites from other towns like the Xius of Uxmal and Cocomes of Mayapán. Regardless of its origin, it is yet another example of the broad differences between Chichén Itza and the traditional Mayan polity[26].

Chapter 4: The Era of Chichén Itza's Glory

According to oral histories collected amongst the Yucatecan Maya in the modern period, Chichén Itza began to peak when its leaders joined up with the Xiu family (the former leaders of Uxmal) to overthrow the Cocomes of Mayapán. Uxmal had been obliterated by Mayapán during a previous war, but now its rulers exacted vengeance. This history is a bit jumbled because the date given for these events is 1436 A.D., long after the archaeological record shows Chichén Itza had risen and fallen,[27] but it is still possible that the general outline of events is correct. If Uxmal/Xiu and Chichén Itza were allies against Mayapán and the Cocomes for dominance of the northern Yucatán, the fighting may represent a breakdown of an earlier confederation[28]. This may also be proof that Chichén Itza was at one point merely an outpost of Toltec culture in the south or as a center for transcontinental trade before becoming a Mayan superpower.

Eventually, however, Chichén Itza rose to prominence and began to exert influence influence on other Mayan city-states and the ways of life of both elites and commoners during its heyday. The easiest indication of the spread of Chichén Itza's influence is the expansion of the cult of Kukulkan throughout the Mayan region. Evidence suggests that the surrounding cities adopted the worship of Kukulkan wholeheartedly; for example, temples were erected in Mayapán and the Spanish documented a grand yearly festival dedicated to the god in the center of Maní, which was run by the Xiu family. Other Postclassic Yucatán cities also developed temples to the god, and even the little walled city of Tulum on the eastern shore had a Temple to the Wind God[29]. In the Highlands, the Qui'che Maya incorporated the "Sovereign Plumed Serpent" into the heart of their mythology as the creator of the world, as written in a sacred book called the *Popol Vuh*. Its opening passage reads in part:

"Whatever there is that might be is simply not there: only the pooled water, only the calm sea, only it alone is pooled. Whatever might be is simply not there: only murmurs, ripples in the dark, in the night. Only the Maker, Modeler alone, Sovereign Plumed Serpent, the Bearers, Begetters are in the water, a glittering light. They are there, they are enclosed in quetzal feathers, in blue-green. Thus the name,

---

26 "Chichen Itza" in *Exploring Mesoamerica* by John M.D. Pohl (1999). Oxford University Press. Pg 129
27 *The Myths of Mexico and Peru* by Lewis Spence. 1913 (2005). Barnes and Noble Books. Pg 135.
28 However, some archaeologists have dated Mayapán as a later city, after the decline of both of its neighbors - the debate is still out.
29 "Zona Arqueológica de Tulum" at the National Institute of Anthropology and History of Mexico Homepage
http://www.inah.gob.mx/index.php?option=com_content&view=article&id=5491

'Plumed Serpent.' They are great knowers, great thinkers in their very being.[30]

Perhaps the most telling evidence of the god's eventual importance comes from the Lacandon Maya, the last non-Christianized Mayan group. The Lacandon Maya continue to practice their ancient religion in their small isolated homesteads deep in the Lacandon jungle on the opposite side of the Highlands from Chichén Itza. These tiny farms are perhaps the most distant spot of the Mayan world from the great pyramid of Kukulkan (El Castillo), yet even here Kukulkan makes an appearance as the flying serpent companion of the sun god[31].

So what was life like in the shadow of the splendor of the Pyramid of Kukulkan? For the elites, it probably seemed to be the center of the universe. Within sight of the pyramid, archaeologists have found a grand market where goods came and went, including local salt, cotton, precious stones, worked copper, gold, tools, cacao, feathers, and furs. The elite no doubt took advantage of this abundant wealth and garbed themselves and their homes in the finest things available. Their homes had large areas for entertaining and were decorated with elaborate frescoes[32], and the Mayan leadership was infamous for their grand parties, including competitive drinking, feasting, and numerous forms of performative art such as dancing, music, jesting, storytelling and theater.

Even more important than mercantile pursuits were the ritual duties. In addition to the Pyramid, there were numerous other temples around the Core, and the elite was expected to participate in elaborate rituals, including bloodletting from early childhood. All Maya gave of their own blood to the gods, but the leaders were held to a higher standard of sacrifice, and this would have been all the more important in Chichén Itza because the city was undoubtedly a center for pilgrimage. The rest of the Mayan world looked to the leaders of Chichén Itza to hold up the standard for appropriate worship of Kukulkan. Thus, moreso than in other cities, the Chichén elite were under even more pressure to perform their ritual duties, not just from their own people but also from foreign observers as well[33].

Given its prestige and the importance of rituals, it is perhaps not surprising that seemingly everyone in the city participated in much of the ritual life. El Castillo appears to have been designed with a broad courtyard at its base so that crowds of spectators could watch, and every kind of inhabitant would have benefited from the presence of a diverse marketplace. Moreover, many were probably proud of their citizenship in what seemed to be the world's mightiest city, and there was no better place to be devoted to the worship of the "Sovereign Plumed Serpent."

That said, the lives of the commoners, who comprised the vast majority of the population even in a wealthy city-state like Chichén Itza, were not nearly as glamorous as those of the leadership. While the archaeology for this group is not as well developed as those of the elite, a lot can be gleaned from the

---

30 *Popol Vuh: The Definitive Edition of the Mayan Book of the Dawn of Life and the Glories of Gods and Kings.* Dennis Tedlock (Trans.) (1996). Touchstone Books. Quote on pg 64

31 *Handbook of Mesoamerican Mythology* by Kay Almere Read and Jason González (2000). Oxford University Press. Pg 201

32 This is an art form with considerable antiquity amongst the Maya; perhaps the most important surviving frescoes are in the ruins of Bonampak.

33 "The Royal Culture of the Maya" in *The Chronicle of the Mayan Kings and Queens: Deciphering the Dynasties of the Ancient Maya* by Simon Martin and Nikolai Grube (2000). Thames and Hudson. Pgs 14-16.

accounts of early Spanish observers. Diego de Landa, the infamous Spanish bishop who burned Maya texts, wrote an elaborate description of the Yucatán to people back home. He described the peasantry as living in wooden homes with whitewashed walls and steeply-pitched thatched roofs. He noted that near their homes, they maintained fields of their own as well as commonly-farmed fields that were controlled by local elites, growing primarily corn (maize) but also cacao, chili peppers and vegetables. In the forests and swamps, they hunted venison, manatees, fish and wild fowl.[34]

De Landa described the traditional male attire, which has been confirmed by comparing it to images in frescoes and books, as "a strip of cloth a hand broad that served for breeches and leggings, and which they wrapped several times about the waist, leaving one end hanging in front and one behind. These ends were embroidered by their wives with much care and with featherwork. They wore large square mantles, which they threw over the shoulders. They wore sandals of hemp or deerskin tanned dry, and then no other garments." The women wore skirts and, in some regions, covered their torsos with doubled-sided mantles they fastened below the armpits. But for others, "their sole garment is a long wide sack, open at the sides, reaching to the thighs and there fastened by its own ends." Even today, the Mayan women are renowned for their embroidery. According to De Landa, Mayan women also had elaborate hairdos, including "coiffures as fine as those of the most coquettish Spanish women", and they decorated themselves with piercings, tattoos, body paint and by filing their teeth. Of course, all of these clothes and decorations were finer and more elaborate amongst the elites than the poor.[35]

As these descriptions make clear, at the height of Chichén Itza's power, the society there was centralized, highly-organized and strictly stratified between social classes. For those who controlled it, Chichén Itza's wealth allowed for incredible displays of power and sophistication. Indeed, the city's leadership developed a standard for ritual and elegance that set the standard for the entire Mayan region and served to promote not only their trading influence but also the cult of Kukulkan. For those at the bottom, life in Chichén Itza was much like the peasant life elsewhere, consisting of long, labor-filled hours on personal and elite-owned plots of land, with small homes and rich family life.

Chapter 5: The Decline of Chichén Itza

Unlike the Mesoamerican cities conquered by the Spanish, like the Incan city of Cuzco and the Aztec city of Tenochtitlan, the fall of Chichén Itza was not documented in any surviving books. It seems the city was not conquered and therefore did not collapse in fire and blood. Instead, it apparently faded away over time and became abandoned, and since this process occurred gradually over an extended period of time, the causes of Chichén Itza's collapse are likely complex and shifting. It also means historians may never be able to determine all of the root causes or understand just how Chichén Itza met its end.

However, it's important not to confuse complexity and obscurity with "mystery." Much has been

---

34 *Yucatan Before and After the Conquest* by Friar Diego de Landa. William Gates (trans.) 1566 (1978). Dover Books. Pgs 32-39, 93-101
35 *Yucatan Before and After the Conquest* by Friar Diego de Landa. William Gates (trans.) 1566 (1978). Dover Books. Pgs 33, 53-54

made in some documentaries and popular writing about "mysterious" places of the ancient past like Chichén Itza, Stonehenge or the Moai of Easter Island, a process that opens the doors for wild theories, such as those that claim El Castillo was dedicated to ancient alien astronauts. While the details of how Chichén Itza was first founded and how it declined are difficult archaeological questions, there is nothing that scholars have encountered in the archaeological record that cannot be understood without relying on extraterrestrial or supernatural explanations. The buildings of Chichén Itza are impressive by any standard, but they're all the more impressive because archaeologists can understand the techniques used by their ancient human builders, and how these designs evolved out of earlier ones. Likewise, elements of the city's decline are still unknown, but there is nothing to suggest abnormal factors were involved. Cities across the world have declined naturally for a variety of reasons, like climate change, military conquest, shifting trade routes, exhausted natural resources, declining harvests, drought, or pestilence. Furthermore, the notion that the Maya were "lost" or disappeared is an absurd one because many Maya still live in the region; in fact, they make up the majority of the population of Guatemala and are considerable minorities in Belize and the Mexican states of Quintana Roo, Yucatán, Campeche, Chiapas and the nation of Belize.

What is known about the decline of Chichén Itza is that the city's dominance over the Mayan world lasted roughly three centuries, from about 900-1200 A.D. It's also known that the Xiu and Cocomes had established a new capital at Mayapán by 1220 A.D., where they created architectural works that mimicked those in Chichén Itza and governed themselves by Mul Tepal ("joint rule"), a confederated system which appears similar to the old Itza system. The decline of the strength of this confederacy continued for hundreds of years, and by 1450, oral history accounts collected by the Spanish documented that the Yucatan Peninsula was divided amongst 16 rival city-states[36].

One of the more important reasons for the decline of Chichén Itza was probably the destruction of its sister-city, Tula. The city had been declining throughout the 12th century, probably due to faltering fertility, and some time in the 1170s (some say 1179 A.D.) it was attacked and looted. Likewise, the intermediate port city connecting the two, el Tajín[37], was also conquered in the late 12th century, making any search for new markets by the Itzaes difficult[38]. The destruction of the northern anchor of their trade system must have had a devastating impact upon Chichén Itza[39]. Not only was Tula the destination of much of their trade and the source of much of their exotic goods, it was also Chichén Itza's religious and political template.

For their part, the Maya themselves tell a tale regarding the proximate cause for Chichén Itza's decline, the story of Canek:

> "A king of Chichén called Canek fell desperately in love iwth a young princess, who, whether she did not return his affection or whether she was compleded ot obey a parental mandate, married a more powerful Yucatec *cacique*. The discarded

36 "Chichen Itza" in *Exploring Mesoamerica* by John M.D. Pohl (1999). Oxford University Press. Pg 129-130
37 The Huaxtecs who had built el Tajín and bridged the Tula-Chichén gap were located in central Mexico but were ethnically and linguistically related to the Maya.
38 "El Tajín" in *Exploring Mesoamerica* by John M.D. Pohl (1999). Oxford University Press. Pg 146-147
39 "Tula" in *Exploring Mesoamerica* by John M.D. Pohl (1999). Oxford University Press. Pg 154-158

lover, unable to bear his loss, and moved by love and despair, armed his dependents and suddenly fell upon his successful rival. Then the gaiety of the feast was exchanged for the din of war, and amidst the confusion, the u Chichén prince disappeared, carrying off the beautiful bride. But conscious that his power was less than his rival's, and fearing his vengeance, he fled the country with most of his vassals."[40]

Of course, this story does not explain the disappearance of what was at one point the mightiest city in the region. For one, it claims that the "king" who ruled Chichén Itza had more powerful enemies, so if that was true, the city was already in decline. It appears probable, however, that there is some kernel of truth here, because it is known that at one point, as the city began to fade, a group of Itzaes fled not only the city but the Lowlands in general. These refugees arrived in an area of modern-day Guatemala and settled on the lake now known as Petén Itza, Guatemala's second-largest lake[41]. By the time the Spanish arrived to the región, the Itzaes still ruled the area from the city of Tayasal[42]. Tayasal was not one of the great Mayan capitals, but it is distinctive for a number of reasons, not the least of which is that it was the last independent Mayan city-state to be conquered by the Spanish. It was built upon an island and was well-fortified and isolated. If Canek and his followers truly built a fortress to protect themselves from the wrath of their enemies, they were at least successful in creating a bastion that outlasted every other.

Today, the last remnant of the Itza' branch of the Mayan language can be found amongst a handful of elderly speakers in the Highlands of Guatemala near Lake Petén Itza. While this is far from the Lowlands, where it was once the tongue of the mighty city-state of Chichén Itza, the language still retains greater similarities to the Lowland languages than it does to its neighboring Mayan dialects, which suggests evidence of ancient migrations that occurred after the fall of Chichén Itza.[43]

So what can be said with certainty about the disappearance of Chichén Itza? The city was founded and located based upon long-distance trade in commodities and ideas, and when those networks collapsed after the destruction of both Tula and El Tajín, the city quickly lost a lot of its relevance. As trade moved in new directions, the wealthy families of the confederacy - the Cocomes and Xiu in particular - were forced to rely upon different sources of power and wealth, placing their emphasis on holdings outside the city. By 1220, about 50 years after the fall of Tula, the center of power was already at Mayapán. This was probably a period of strife between elite families seeking to maintain (or increase) their power in a shifting political and economic landscape, and this may explain why elites like Canek retreated up into the Highlands to establish a new Itza city on the shores of Lake Petén Itza. The old city was never completely abandoned, as it continued to be used for ritual purposes until the arrival of the Spanish, but it slowly faded with fewer and fewer families living in what was increasingly a ruin swallowed up by the jungle.

---

40 *The Myths of Mexico and Peru* by Lewis Spence. 1913 (2005). Barnes and Noble Books. Pg 165.
41 *The Myths of Mexico and Peru* by Lewis Spence. 1913 (2005). Barnes and Noble Books. Pg 136.
42 "A Peninsula That May Have Been an Island: Tayasal, Peten, Guatemala" by Ruben E. Reina. In the journal *Expedition*, Fall 1966. Pg 16 - 29. Accessed online at: http://www.penn.museum/documents/publications/expedition/PDFs/9-1/Reina.pdf
43 "Itza': A Language of Guatemala" in the Ethnologue. Accessed online at: http://www.ethnologue.com/language/itz

Even still, the last non-Catholicized Maya group, the Lacandon of Chiapas, regularly traveled to the nearby ruin of Bonampak, where they performed rituals within the ancient, ruined temples. This suggests they had an unbroken tradition of prayer and ritual that dated back to the time when the city was inhabited[44]. Likewise, there are accounts of the ruins of Uxmal being used by the powerful Xiu family (said to be descendants of the former rulers) and rituals occuring at Chichén Itza even after the Spanish Conquest. Presumably, they took a form similar to that of the Lacandon: reverential entry into a site associated with both gods and ancestors, and then sacrifices and prayers made in crumbling temples and altars. It's possible the ruined state of the buildings became integrated into the religious lore itself, with the buildings becoming associated with a golden age of mythic ancestors worthy of veneration. In fact, Bishop Landa, the Spaniard sent to Christianize the Maya, ordered a cannon (and probably guards) to be placed on top of El Castillo to prevent just such activity.

Thus, even though Chichén Itza declined, it continued to be a part of the sacred landscape and then bécame a landscape of folklore. In other words, Chichén Itza never vanished from the Yucatec Mayan memory. During the "Talking Cross" revolts, part of the larger Mayan Caste War (1847-1901) against Mestizo domination, prophecies held that the rise of the revolt must include the rebels "reaching an agreement with the governor who lives in the ruins," an idea which was "a reference to the legendary Itza king promised in the books of *Chilam Balam*"[45].

Chapter 6: The "Discovery" of the Ruins and Their Modern Fame

The ancient Maya were "rediscovered" by the West in the mid-19th century when the writings of de Landa and other Spaniards came to the attention of an English-speaking public fascinated with the emerging field of archaeology. Eventually, a search for the city and other Yucatecan ruins was launched by John Lloyd Stephens and Frederick Catherwood, an American and Englishman. Stephens and Catherwood captured European and Euro-American imaginations with their book *Incidents of Travel in Yucatan* (1841), which came out just before the 1847 Caste War in the Yucatán. It was known for the intricate detail and great beauty of Catherwood's images of the ruins, which are sometimes still used by scholars who seek to understand details of the buildings that have eroded in the century and a half since publication[46]. This was the era of grand expeditions and public fascination with the concept of lost cities, and the book became a best-seller.

The area became inaccessible again at the start of the 1847 war and remained so until the war's conclusion in 1901, but this was soon followed up by the Mexican Revolution of 1910-1920. After the Revolution, the new Institutional Revolutionary Party (PRI) government established a different relationship with the Pre-Columbian past. This government was staunchly nationalist and viewed modern-day Mexico as a Mestizo state, a nation that was equally Spanish and indigenous in origin. Thus, Mexico's Pre-Columbian ruins were transformed from being crumbling heathen relics, which for centuries were considered best left to looters and the dead, into a source of pride and identity for the nation. At Chichén Itza, this new interest took the form of a flurry of archaeological excavation and a

---

44 *Life, Ritual and Religion Among the Lacandon Maya* by R. Jon McGee (1990). Wadsworth Publishing.
45 *The Caste War of the Yucatán* by Nelson A. Reed (2001). Stanford University Press. Pg 154.
46 "Frederick Catherwood's Lithographs" accessed online at: http://www.casa-catherwood.com/catherwoodinenglish.html

major government-sponsored restoration of the jungle-covered El Castillo pyramid, with a parallel restoration of the nearby Temple of Warriors by the U.S.-based Carnegie Institution, both during the 1920s and 30s. This was followed in the 1930s by another government-sponsored excavation, this time into the side of the Castillo. That excavation discovered the two earlier pyramids buried under its surface. Excavations and restorations have continued in the decades since then, including impressive dredging of the Sacred Cenote in the 1950s[47].

Photo of a throne depicting a jaguar, found inside El Castillo

Chichén Itza is currently protected and managed under a 1972 law whose name translates in English as "*Federal Law on Monuments and Archaeological, Artistic and Historic Zones.*" Under the provisions of that statute, the president declared the ruins an "archaeological monument" in 1986, which places the site under the management of the National Institute of Anthropology and History (INAH) based in Mexico City. In 1987, the state of Yucatan - where the ruins are located - created its own unique Board of Units of Cultural and Tourism Services, which oversees the conservation and touristic promotion of all of the major archaeological sites within the region.[48]

Chichén Itza received further recognition in 1988 when Mexico requested its inscription on the list of World Heritage Sites. This list, which includes the Taj Mahal and the royal palace at Versailles, catalogues the most significant locations in world history and culture, as well as the Earth's most precious natural locations. The significance of the site for the Mexican people is indicated by the fact that it was part of only the second group of sites submitted by their government for inscription.[49]

47 *Metals from the Cenote of Sacrifice: Chichen Itza, Yucatan* by S.K. Lothrop (1952). The Cambridge Museum.
48 "Pre-Hispanic City of Chichen Itza" at the UNESCO World Heritage List, accessed online at: http://whc.unesco.org/en/list/483

This promotion, aided by the site's photogenic ruins, has led to Chichén Itza becoming one of the region's premier tourist sites, attracting between 3,500-8,000 visitors a day. In fact, the splendor of El Castillo has made it a stand-in for the entire nation of Mexico in tourism campaigns for years. However, the affection for Chichén Itza is not something simply manufactured for tourism either, as it has long since become a point of Mexican pride since the 1920 revolution. The depth of this feeling was seen in 2007, when the "New7Wonders" Foundation began an international contest in which the public was invited to vote on a new list of "Seven Wonders of the World." All of the winners achieved their status in part through a public (typically government-sponsored) campaign, and Mexicans voted in droves for Chichén Itza, putting it ahead of Mexico's other impressive ruins[50].

Ironically, it is this love that is today the greatest threat to the conservation of the site. While made of stone, much of the structure of the buildings is reconstructed and relatively fragile when under stress. In 2006, tourists were no longer allowed to climb the Castillo, and in 2011 INAH asked for the increased number of visitors coming to view the shadows move on the Castillo on the equinox to remain off of all of the structures and avoid other activities that have the potential to damage the site[51].

Another threat comes from the increasing presence of acid rain in the region. The reason why elaborate carvings survived to be recorded by Frederick Catherwood in the 19th century yet decomposed so quickly in the late 19th and early 20th centuries is largely due to the increased acidity in the rainfall throughout the Yucatán Peninsula. Since the structures are built of limestone (like the Peninsula itself), they are particularly susceptible to erosion, and an increasing amount of detail has permanently disappeared from the buildings' facades. For instance, by the late 1980s, a black crust of acid deposit covered an entire wall of the Grand Ballcourt in the city[52].

The final challenge facing the ruins currently is a growing conflict over who controls the ruins. After the Mexican Revolution, the government - along with the majority of Mestizos in central Mexico - came to view the ancient ruins as an example of shared national patrimony to be protected by the central state. However, the local Maya have increasingly asserted that these sites were not created by the ancestors of the Mestizos (who, if they have indigenous ancestry, tend to be from groups like the Aztec from central Mexico) but instead by their ancestors. While INAH recognizes this special relationship in a small way by allowing Maya to enter the ruins without paying fees, the locals push for greater benefits. At Chichén Itza, this has created a conflict over whether, how many and where Maya artisans can sell their handicrafts to tourists, and this reached a head in 2006 when Subcomandante Marcos, the spokesman of the Zapatista revolutionary group (EZLN), came to Chichén Itza. The EZLN represents Mayan communities in the state of Chiapas who had reached out to their Yucatecan cousins and sent Marcos to the state of Yucatán. The fact that the site remains potent enough that a

49 "Pre-Hispanic City of Chichen Itza" at the UNESCO World Heritage List, accessed online at:
   http://whc.unesco.org/en/list/483
50 "Chichen Itza among New 7 Wonders of the World" by Suzanne Barbezat. Accessed online at:
   http://gomexico.about.com/b/2007/07/09/chichen-itza-among-new-7-wonders-of-the-world.htm
51 "Mexican Pyramids Under Threat from Equinox Revellers" by Robin Yapp for *The Telegraph* accessed online at:
   http://www.telegraph.co.uk/news/worldnews/centralamericaandthecaribbean/mexico/8390686/Mexican-pyramids-under-threat-from-Equinox-revellers.html
52 "New Threat to Maya Ruins: Acid Rain" by John Noble Wilford, for the *New York Times* Aug 8, 1989. Accessed online
   at :http://www.nytimes.com/1989/08/08/science/new-threat-to-maya-ruins-acid-rain.html?pagewanted=all&src=pm

world-renowned Mayan revolutionary will visit over a debate regarding vendors' rights is evidence of the increasingly contested nature of this particular space[53].

Elaborately carved masks that show signs of weatherization

Thus stands Chichén Itza at the dawn of the new millennium. It is a proud and ancient city, increasingly better understood by scholars (if not always the general public),but weathering around the edges. It also stands squarely within the crosshairs of a struggle over the patrimony of Mexico, a debate that reverberates around the world as indigenous peoples and national governments grapple over control, interpretation and profit of heritage sites.

Bibliography

Andrews, Anthony P.; E. Wyllys Andrews V, and Fernando Robles Castellanos (January 2003). "The Northern Maya Collapse and its Aftermath". Ancient Mesoamerica (New York: Cambridge University Press)

Aveni, Anthony F. (1997). Stairways to the Stars: Skywatching in Three Great Ancient Cultures. New York: John Wiley & Sons.

---

53 "Marcos Rips Up Script: 'We're Going to Chichen Itzá" by Al Giordano Jan 20, 2006. Accessed online at: http://www.narconews.com/Issue40/article1570.html

Brunhouse, Robert (1971). Sylvanus Morley and the World of the Ancient Mayas. Norman, Oklahoma: University of Oklahoma Press.

Charnay, Désiré (1887). Ancient Cities of the New World: Being Voyages and Explorations in Mexico and Central America from 1857–1882. J. Gonino and Helen S. Conant (trans.). New York: Harper & Brothers.

Coe, Michael D. (1999). The Maya. Ancient peoples and places series (6th edition, fully revised and expanded ed.). London and New York: Thames & Hudson.

Coggins, Clemency Chase (1984). Cenote of Sacrifice: Maya Treasures from the Sacred Well at Chichén Itza. Austin, TX: University of Texas Press.

Colas, Pierre R.; and Alexander Voss (2006). "A Game of Life and Death – The Maya Ball Game". In Nikolai Grube (ed.). Maya: Divine Kings of the Rain Forest. Eva Eggebrecht and Matthias Seidel (assistant eds.). Cologne, Germany: Könemann. pp. 186–191. ISBN 978-3-8331-1957-6. OCLC 71165439.

Demarest, Arthur (2004). Ancient Maya: The Rise and Fall of a Rainforest Civilization. Case Studies in Early Societies, No. 3. Cambridge: Cambridge University Press.

Miller, Mary Ellen (1999). Maya Art and Architecture. London and New York: Thames & Hudson.

Perry, Richard D. (ed.) (2001). Exploring Yucatan: A Traveler's Anthology. Santa Barbara, CA: Espadaña Press.

Phillips, Charles (2006, 2007). The Complete Illustrated History of the Aztecs & Maya: The definitive chronicle of the ancient peoples of Central America & Mexico - including the Aztec, Maya, Olmec, Mixtec, Toltec & Zapotec. London: Anness Publishing Ltd. ISBN 1-84681-197-X. OCLC 642211652.

Schele, Linda; and David Freidel (1990). A Forest of Kings: The Untold Story of the Ancient Maya (Reprint ed.). New York: Harper Perennial.

Sharer, Robert J.; with Loa P. Traxler (2006). The Ancient Maya (6th (fully revised) ed.). Stanford, CA: Stanford University Press.

Thompson, J. Eric S. (1966). The Rise and Fall of Maya Civilization. Norman, Oklahoma: University of Oklahoma Press.